WHERE ARE YOU LOKU?

BY

SUSAN FARRUGIA

CONTENTS

PSALM 27

The LORD is my light and my salvation; whom shall I fear? The LORD is the stronghold of my life;of whom shall I be afraid? One thing have I asked of the LORD, that will I seek after; that I may dwell in the house of the LORD all the days of my life, to behold the beauty of the LORD, and to inquire in his temple. For he will hide me in his shelter in the day of trouble; he will conceal me under the cover of his tent, he will set me high upon a rock. Hear, O LORD, when I cry aloud, be gracious to me and answer me! Thou hast said, Seek ye my face, My heart says to thee, Thy face, LORD, do I seek. Hide not thy face from me. each me thy way, O LORD; and lead me on a level path because of my enemies.

Wait for the LORD; be strong, and let your heart take courage; yea, wait for the LORD!

(Ps 27: 1, 4-6, 8 11, 14)

INTRODUCTION

Have we not, in any time in our lives, found ourselves in a situation emotionally distraught or spiritually vulnerable and cried out for the help of the Lord? We have cried out for his help and presence, for we have felt alone. This does not mean that we are alone, for he said he will never leave us alone and he will be with us until the end of time. But let us be sincere, what we feel and what actual is, are not always the same. The Lord is always with us and we are called to believe his Word. Our husbands, wives, children, friends and family cannot be with us all the time. They cannot take care of us, protect us nor guide us all the time, but the Lord can.

I hope that these stories may throw some light on certain situations we may find ourselves in and reveal a way in which the Lord may be speaking to us. The best way is always to spend time in his Presence, to immerse yourself in His Word and to allow the Holy Spirit to open your heart and mind to Him.

God bless you always – Sue

CHAPTER ONE

I AM FRIGHTENED LORD,
WHERE ARE YOU?

Martha rushed out of the door fast, she had to hurry. The wind was whipping up, for a rough storm was looming. She and Laura had been studying for their end of year exams, but she had to get home fast before it began to rain heavily. Already the clouds were gathering in the sky, it was getting dark, small droplets began to fall and she knew that soon it would be raining buckets. Martha quickened her step. "Lord help me" she prayed. Martha had to cross the small wooden bridge that lay between her own home and Laura's home. As she approached the stream, she could already see the stream was filling up and flowing strongly. The clouds darkened and the rain began to fall heavily. Martha was getting wet, her overcoat did not offer much protection against the rain. Nothing for it, she had to continue. She came to the bridge. The water was now touching the bridge. She had to cross that bridge. Now with the rising water the solid bridge seemed rickety, as though it were to collapse at any moment.

She placed a foot on the bridge and gently began to walk across.

Her feet were being soaked by the water that came over the bridge. The bridge held a while but she felt it shudder under her. "I am frightened Lord – where are you?" she cried out. Suddenly she felt a strong hand underneath her elbow holding her firm. "I am here, don't be afraid" said the man "I'll help you across". Martha had not noticed the man at all, and was rather shaken and frightened that he had come up behind her like that.

Yet his voice so strong and gentle gave her courage. She let him hold her. Gently he swung her up and carried her across the bridge as light as a feather, laying her down on firm though wet ground on the other side. The rain was by now pelting down. She was soaked through. "Thank you, sir" she said "Martha I'll see you home safely" the man said. He walked with her, their feet slushing in the sodden ground. He put his arms and overcoat over her as though to protect and cover her. As they walked, he spoke to her, asking about her studies and family life. When he smiled, his eyes beamed knowingly and his mouth curled up. Her mind was racing – now who did this man remind her of? She had never met him, this she knew, but somehow it was like she had always known him. He seemed that he knew her. She could not figure it out at all!

The sky was dark and it was now night. The clouds had dispersed a bit and the moon had come out and the stars shone, sparkling in the darkened sky. The rain had ceased a bit. Slowly Martha had arrived home. She ran up the stairs of the porch. Her mother and father were there, worried out of their wits for their daughter. She told them that this man met her on the way and had brought her home. They turned to the man to thank him and ask him in for supper, and to warm himself up a bit. He was thankful but declined the offer for supper. He was only glad that she was safely home. Martha turned around to speak to him but he was gone, he was nowhere to be found. Martha ran out to look for him. He had disappeared as suddenly as he had appeared. This was so strange, a tight knot twisted in her guts. She went inside. Her mother helped her out of her sodden clothes and gave her a hot bowl of vegetable soup. Martha recounted the adventure she had on the way. As she spoke, she remembered the small details she had not noticed. "How did he know her name?" He seemed to know everything about her? She remembered the light in his eyes and the curl of his mouth as he spoke – the sense of knowing him but could not understand where.

What was strange was though she was soaked through to the bone, he was not, not even his overcoat was wet, and though they were sloshing in the mud, his boots remained clean! Hers were soaked through. This was just so bewildering. Martha shrugged it all off, maybe she was just imagining things. Her parents had never seen the man before, he was not from any neighbouring farm or village., but they were grateful that he just happened to come along when he did to help their Martha.

After supper, Martha went up to bed. As she lay in bed, the wind brushed the branches against her window. She looked out and she could swear that she could see the face of the man smiling out there, looking up at her, speaking to her. "Do not be afraid, I am with you always Martha, with you, where ever you go and where ever you are!"

Martha went to bed and prayed – "thank you Lord for the man you sent to help me home today". In her heart she heard these words from Ps 91.

> He will cover you with his pinions,
> and under his wings you will find refuge;

his faithfulness is a shield and buckler. You will not fear the

terror of the night,

or the pestilence that stalks in darkness.

For he will command his angels concerning you

to guard you in all your ways.

On their hands they will bear you up,

so that you will not dash your foot against a stone.

Because he cleaves to me in love, I will deliver him;

I will protect him, because he knows my name.

When he calls to me, I will answer him;

I will be with him in trouble,

I will rescue him and honor him. (Ps 91: 4-14)

She knew that the Lord had answered her prayer when in her fear she cried out for help. He had sent one of his angels to care and watch over her, to bring her safely home. This angel would always be with her to care and watch over her.

So, to each one of us, the Lord has placed a guardian angel. He is there, by the Lord's choosing to watch over us, to lead and to guide us during the day and the night. Let him walk with you.

CHAPTER TWO
I AM ANGRY LORD,
WHERE ARE YOU?

Mark opened the door of his home. His father lay on the couch with his head in his hands and his mother over the cooker, cooking, crying at the same time.

"Hey mum, dad, I'm home. What's happened?" Mark saw both his parents very upset. His father Donald turned to his son and said, "Mark, I've lost my job, we have until the end of the month here as we cannot pay the rent on just your mother's wage. We are being evicted from here".

Mark who was just 13 years old, was furious "how can they do this? Its Christmas eve – how can they do this?" He was so upset, he ran outside and downstairs. He went outside onto the street. His parents called after him, but Mark just ran out crying and angry. The snow began to fall gently creating a fairylike white on the ground "it's Christmas" cried Mark "and they do this, Lord it's not fair, I am angry Lord, where are you?"

Quietly and gently sobbing Mark walked not really knowing where he was going. In the far distance he could hear Christmas carols, they sounded familiar and comforting so he walked in their direction. The Christmas carols were coming from St Mary's Church. He arrived there and entered. The Church door was open with lights at the entrance. The choir were singing near the altar. On the left was a large Christmas tree adorned with so many lights and on the right was a crib with the baby Jesus, Mary and Joseph, the scene of Bethlehem. Mark went in and sat in the back pew. With his head in his hands he began to sob. "Why Lord, why? I am angry Lord, help me, where are you?"

Mark didn't notice Fr James come towards him. He sat down next to him and putting his arm around him said "Mark, son what is it?' Mark told him and also how he felt. He felt ashamed that he was angry – "I want to confess my anger Father, but I am very angry. People are cruel and on Christmas Eve too! My parents are distraught and I do not know what to do."

Fr James held Mark close, come let us pray Mark "Eternal Father, in you all things are possible take the anger of this child Mark and work all things for the good for those who love you. Nothing is impossible for you. When you close a door, you open another in front.

We ask you Father in the name of Jesus your beloved son to help Mark and his family this Christmas. Amen."

"Is that ok Mark" said Fr James. "Yes Father" said Mark, "I already feel a bit better I guess I have to trust in Jesus!".

Mark went out waving goodbye to Fr James and genuflected on going out of the church. The snow was beginning to fall heavily outside. Mark pulled his coat around him. The Christmas carols were such a comfort as the voices lofted from the church and the outside area.

Mark began to walk home but this time went through the high street where the shops were, perhaps the sight of Christmas decorations would cheer him up. A Father Christmas, all dressed up was ringing his bell and crying "Ho Ho Ho!" Mark laughed "some ho ho ho it is this year!" he commented. Passing by the One in All General Store, Mr Evans came out "Mark, come in here, there is something I want to show you!" Mark went in not knowing what to expect "Mark I want you to choose any toy you want from the store, any toy." "Sir, I do not have the money to pay you." "That's ok" said Mr Evans, "it's my gift to you" Mark was overjoyed, Mark looked around. He had for a long time had his eye on the red fire engine.

"Can I take the red fire engine please Mr Evans. I will work for it. Promise?" "it's my gift to you" said Mr Evans kindly.

Mark was so excited, he took the fire engine and held it close to him as though it were going to run away, but as he was walking out of the shop, he stopped in his tracks and returned. "Mr Evans, I cannot take the fire engine, I would rather take a gift for my dad and mum instead, if it's ok with you? I will work for it. Promise". Mr Evans saw the goodness of the boy's heart.

"Mark choose what you want for your mother and father". Mark chose the silver beads his mother had always admired when passing the store and a shining watch for his dad – they could never afford them. "I'll pay you for these Mr Evans, promise." "Yes, you can work for them, if you wish". Mark was overjoyed, "Yes, I will work for them" Mark looked around.

"You can have these and the fire engine Mark – and yes you can work for them after school, mind you after your studies ok, we cannot have you missing out on your schoolwork. You can help me clear the store after a day's work and put out the trash ok."

"Yes sir" said Mark, totally overjoyed.

"Now give me these items let me gift wrap them for you, it is Christmas after all"

"Thank you, Mr. Evans, thank you Lord!" His parents could never afford to buy such things and now even though they were going under, the Lord was helping them "thank you Lord." Mark's heart sang with gratitude

Excitedly Mark rushed out of the store holding his new found treasure trove "Thank you Mr Evans and a Merry Christmas to you sir!" Maybe it was not going to be such a bad Christmas after all.

Mark began to walk down the High Street. On the corner near the supermarket he saw a mother and her little son, he was crying. Mark stopped, "what's wrong m'am can I help you?" "Thank you, son", the woman said, "but my son would very much like the fire truck in Mr Evan's store and I just cannot afford to buy it!" Mark knew instinctively what he had to do. Although he had wanted the fire engine so much, he held out the fire engine and gave it to the boy.

"Here take it, have it. I am giving it to you". The little boy's eyes shone and he beamed. "why thank you, this is just so kind of you. But please, this is yours!"

"No M'am, allow me to give it to your little boy for   Christmas"

"You are so kind young man, may the Lord bless you for your kindness!' The woman hugged him. The little boy was overjoyed, and hugged Mark. "Thank you", he cried, "thank you."

Mark walked on and was surprised that he was not dismayed that he had given the fire engine away. Instead he felt a deep warmth and glow within him, a sense of well-being. He knew he had done the right thing.

Mark ran home, running up the stairs and dashed into his flat.

"Where have you been Mark Harrison? We have been worried about you!" said Jennie his mother.

Mark told them how upset he was and how he walked toward the Church of St Mary, there he had heard the Christmas carols and he walked in and sitting in the back pew he wept, angry, angry at everyone, angry at the Lord and angry at himself for being angry.

He then told them that Fr James came and spoke to him. He had gone to confession and Fr James prayed for them.

Suddenly as though he just remembered Mark brought out the gifts he had, "oh yes I brought these for you – happy Christmas mum, happy Christmas dad". Mark gave them the presents, so excited. "I had a red fire engine for me, but I gave it to a little boy instead!"

"Now where did you get these, son?" said his father, "you know we cannot afford these things, where did you get the money?"

Mark explained about Mr Evans and the deal they made, he was going to keep his end of the deal. "Dad I promise I will do good, you'll see" Mark's parents looked at their son with love and pride "the Lord has blessed us with a good boy, you are a gift to us Mark".

Suddenly there was a knocking at the door. Donald looked at Jennie, we are not expecting anyone this evening? He opened the door.

A man stood outside "excuse me, Mr Harrison? Donald Harrison please?"

"Yes" said Donald

"Sorry, this is my wife Jennie and our son Mark, please do come in."

The man walked in.

"I am Adam Lawrence of Lawrence Construction Co Ltd, we are doing the restorations at St Mary's Church. It just so happened that Fr James was speaking to me and I mentioned to him that I need a maintenance engineer. He mentioned you. I was wondering if you were interested and available for the post. We have a flat that goes with the job which is rent free, all amenities included? Are you interested? The work and flat is at Bennington Buildings, Bennington Road."

Donald smiled "Am I interested? yes of course! I am free to start straight away"

"That is wonderful" said Mr Lawrence, "we can sort out the paper work the day after Christmas, Boxing Day. Please come to my office at Lawrence Construction Tower in Bennington Road."

"Oh yes, before I forget, I believe I have this for you Mark" Mr Lawrence held out a shining red fire engine to Mark. "This is for you, young man."

Mark just stared at Mr Lawrence incredulously. How and when did he know? He could not have known?

Mr Lawrence turned to leave. The two men shook hands. "So, I will see you Boxing day. A blessed Christmas to you all." He turned and left.

Jennie started to laugh and cry at the same time, Mark was overwhelmed "Wow the Lord sure answers prayers, Thank you Lord."

Donald proclaimed "Come family this is Christmas Eve. We are going to midnight Mass to thank the Lord for his goodness to us."

Hurriedly they put on their coats, scarfs and head coverings and went out holding hands and praising the Lord.

In all things we Praise and Thank God for he works all things for the good for those who love him (Rm 8: 28)

These are the words of him who is holy and true, who holds the key of David. What he opens no one can shut, and what he shuts no one can open. (Rev 3: 7). For when the Lord closes a door behind you, he will open a door in front of you.

Mark walked briskly in the cold night air, his breath creating clouds from his mouth. Mark looked up at the night sky, the stars were shining and twinkling but one particular star shone in a brilliance that was not usual. "Is that the Christmas Star?" thought Mark. He continued to gaze at it. Suddenly it seemed to wink at him. Mark laughed, "Yes, Thankyou, Lord!" and winked back at him!

CHAPTER THREE

I CANNOT FORGIVE,
LORD WHERE ARE YOU?

Simon slammed his fist on the desk. "How could you Brian? How could you? We've been friends for I don't know how long. I brought you into my father's partnership and then you do this? How could you betray me like this?"

Simon was seething with rage. Brian had a work commitment within the firm and in those contacts made different arrangements that would profit him personally. Simon found out and was furious. He was not furious because Brian had done some other work, but because he had betrayed the trust they had between them.

Simon and Brian were at High School together and then at University studying law. Suddenly Brian's dad died of a heart attack, so Simon's father took Brian under his wing and gave him a place in their lawyers' firm with his son Simon. Simon and Brian were like brothers. They had then wanted to make Brian a partner in the firm. Brian was slowly working himself up in the company. Now this!

Simon could not believe it – Brian would not do something like this! When he found out through some documents that somehow came into his hands, he was livid and so sad. He could not forgive him. Their relationship was broken.

Brian stood their motionless in front of Simon as Simon ranted on and on, banging his fist continuously on the desk. The staff outside were silent, afraid to look in through the glass partitions – no-one stirred.

Simon looked at Brian. "You have given me no option Brian. Clear your office and leave now. Now please, Brian! Just go!"

Brian turned and walked out of Simon's office without looking at any of the staff as he walked past them for the shame he felt. He would not be able to live this down. What would he tell his wife Laura? She and Simon's wife, Evelyn were best friends too, rather like sisters as he and Simon were, or had been! How could Simon forgive him? He had made a grave mistake and was now paying a very hefty price for it. What a fool he was, what a fool!

When Brian left Simon's office, Simon called out for a cup of coffee. Janice his secretary came in bringing a cup of steaming black coffee. She did not utter a word, she knew what was best.

Simon began to pace his office, rubbing his head and slamming his fist on the desk. "Damn everything. He could not, would not forgive him – how dare he do this?"

Simon quickly drank the coffee and charged out of the office. He gave instructions to Janice that no-one, but no-one, not even the cleaner was to enter into his office.

Simon went out of the building into the cold winter night air. It was brisk. Perhaps a good walk would help. He walked along the outer lanes of the park, people were jogging and some cycling.

His route had to take him past Brian's house. He walked past not even wanting to look towards the house, but he could not help himself. Funny! the car was not there. Brian should have been home by now.

Simon continued to walk. "Lord we need to talk! You know the situation, but you also know that I just cannot forgive Brian, it's absolutely out of the question after what he has done" Simon walked past the Church, he was drawn to step inside. When inside, he gazed at the Crucifix "why can you not forgive Simon? Have I not forgiven you countless times?" "I too was betrayed, yet I forgave, Simon, in me you can forgive. I never said it would be easy but with my help you can find the heart and will to forgive and to have the relationship restored. Nothing is impossible if you want it badly enough and will allow me to help you Simon!"

Simon cried out "Lord I cannot forgive, where are you Lord, help me Lord!"

Simon sat there gazing and weeping before the crucifix. Never in all his life had he felt the desperation of such a loss. He felt he had lost not a friend but a brother.

"Help me Lord to forgive. Help me. Give me the strength to forgive Brian!"

Simon calmed down and got up, walked out of the Church on his way home. He still remained perplexed why Brian had not yet come home.

Simon opened the front door. Evelyn ran down the stairs crying and calling out "Simon Simon! It's Brian, he's had a bad accident. A car drove into him, a head on collision. He's at the Central Hospital. Laura is there too." Simon called out to the boys "Stay home boys, your mum and I are going down to see what has happened to uncle Brian. Geoffrey take care of the others ok and don't quarrel!"

Quickly Simon and Evelyn jumped into her car and drove to the hospital. "Where's your car Simon?" "I decided to walk it as it seemed fresh tonight" replied Simon.

Arriving at the hospital they rushed in and asked for Brian at the reception. "He is in Casualty, room 7" they answered. Brian and Evelyn ran and found his room. Quietly Simon knocked on the door. Laura quickly opened "Come Simon and Evelyn, thank you for coming."

Simon ran to Brian "hey how are you? What happened?" Brian felt abashed and looked the other way. Simon whispered "it's ok Brian, you'll be ok, what ever you need we will take care of it. The company will cover you. Just get back on your feet again. We need you back with us, we want you back with us!" Brian had tears falling down his face. Simon leaned over, weeping quietly, and held him close "I love you Brian, you are my brother, all is ok, we'll sort it all out ok don't you worry."

Simon and Brian looked at each other and held hands. Laura and Evelyn embraced each other. Simon looked at Laura and told her "Laura don't worry about the expenses. The company insurance will cover you ok. You just make sure that this man gets all the love, attention and care he needs. We will have a lot to celebrate when you get out Brian, a lot to celebrate.

CHAPTER FOUR

THEY HAVE HURT ME LORD,
WHERE ARE YOU LORD?

The clock alarm shrilled in her ears. Sarah reached out her hand to shut it down. It was 6.30 am. She sat up and dragged herself out of bed. Another week at school. She had been going to Thornton High School for a while now, it was horrible. Most of the girls were ok but there was this bunch of them who were nothing but bullies who went out of their way to make her life a misery.

Sarah went to the bathroom and then dressed. Today a new girl was coming in, very likely to their class. Sarah had never met her but she was determined to befriend her and help her through the ropes of settling down, especially if those 5 girls were around.

Once dressed, Sarah ran down into the kitchen where her mum had prepared a coffee and breakfast. "Come good morning Sarah. Have your breakfast, we need to reach school before the traffic starts" said her mother. Her mother worked in the Town's local Library as a Librarian, so she would have to be in before 9.00am.

Sarah was quiet in the car wondering what the day would bring. She raised her heart in prayer, not just for herself but for the new girl. She could not wait to get out of Thornton High. Those girls were becoming a nightmare. "Mary mother help me!" "Lord they are hurting me, where are you Lord?"

Sarah's mother dropped Sarah off at the school gate "I'll pick you up at 3.30 as usual ok Sarah – have a good day!" "Yes mum' said Sarah. "A good day, how does one have a good day here" she mused.

Sarah turned and walked down the school path towards the main door. Near the steps she saw a girl whom she had never met, those 5 girls were laughing at her, taunting her and mocking her. She must be the new girl. Sarah was furious "leave her alone you bullies!" "oh! here comes the goodie goodie!" they swanked and walked off. Sarah turned to the girl and introduced herself. "what were they saying?" Sarah asked. Then then girl lifted her foot. She had a brace on her legs. "one leg is shorter than the other, I have to wear leg braces and special shoes" she said with tears running down her eyes. "those girls are really mean, by the way my name is Janice, thank you for coming when you did!"

Sarah held her arm, "can you walk up those stairs? We can go the other way where there is a slope to walk up." "No! it's fine" said Janice "I can manage these stairs."

Sarah asked her "do you know which class you are in?"

"It 4 A" said Janice. "oh! Great, that's with me, we are in the same class, you can stick around with me, I'll help you" said Sarah. The two new friends smiled and went into the class room.

The teacher was already in class "Ah so this is our new student, Janice Harper I believe, welcome Janice, Sarah will you please show her to her desk, that one near the window, three rows down. Is that ok with you Janice?" Sarah walked with her. All the girls were looking at Janice, many were smiling but the horrible 5 were sniggering together 'enough of that!" retorted the teacher.

Janice sat at her desk and brought out her books. Sarah's desk was next to hers. "It'll be ok don't you worry".

The class started and the morning rolled on. However, every time Janice looked out of the window, she saw a woman walking up and down the school lawn. She pointed this out to Sarah. Sarah looked outside and saw nothing. "Sorry Janice, but I cannot see any woman at all, perhaps you were imagining." Janice was dismayed, she was sure she saw a woman outside.

During the lunch break Sarah and Janice went out and sat on a bench on the front school lawn. Again, the girls came to taunt both Sarah and Janice. "Oh, so now they are buddy buddies, goodie goodies. We are going to have sports day soon, what race will you enter? The limping race?" the girls laughed out loud and went off sniggering.

Janice looked at them in unbelief "where did those creatures come from, what hole did they come out of?" "They do the same to me Janice because I sometimes lisp, take no notice of them it would be better."

During afternoon classes Janice found herself gazing out of the window in search of the woman. "She must be somewhere!" she thought. Suddenly she saw her and pulled Sarah, "look, there is the woman, can you see her now?" Sarah saw her "I've never seen her before, so she cannot be a teacher from here, I wonder who she is?" The woman was wearing a long dress with a shawl around her shoulders.

As they were leaving school, the girls were excited, talking about this woman they had seen. The bullies noted their interaction and tried to pull their attention away with their nasty comments, but they had no effect. Sarah and Janice walked to the school gates to wait for their mums to collect them. On the way home, both of them recounted their sighting of this mysterious woman. When they arrived home, Sarah immediately phoned Janice and they chatted away trying to decipher who she could be. Was she an inspector from the school council, from the town board of schools, was she a new teacher who was to come next year? Her clothes were not up mode fashion, but there again, people can dress as they want, she was modest after all. There were so many questions that were obviously left unanswered. Both Sarah and Janice were left none the wiser.

The next day Sarah and Janice sat looking out of the window to see if they could see the woman again. Sure enough, she was there walking on the school lawn, but this time the woman began to make her way down the path to the lower lawn.

During the first break, Sarah told Janice "look there is the lower lawn, we can go and have our lunch break there, maybe we will meet the woman there, who knows, and find out who she is?" Naturally Janice was all for it. So, at lunch break the girls walked down to the lower lawn. There was no sign of the woman. They sat down on a bench and began to eat their lunch. Suddenly they saw the woman approach them from the lower end of the path. The girls stood up excitedly. The woman approached them and asked if she could join them. They were so excited that they were both tongue-tied. The woman sat down and introduced herself as Miriam. The girls introduced themselves. They asked her who she was, was she a new school teacher, a council board inspector?

The woman smiled and said she was neither. The girls giggled, their presumption was wrong. Soon they began chatting about daily things. The girls mentioned their studies and families. The woman smiled gently. But Janice's face then turned a bit sour, "you see there are these girls who are nothing but bullies, they are so mean with Sarah and me, I have braces on my legs which does not make things any easier. If you were a school inspector, then you could kind of see into this?" She said. "I don't have to be an inspector to see into this" the woman replied to Janice.

Miriam smiled and got up to go. "I have to go now. If you want, we can meet here for lunch break tomorrow ok?" the girls were thrilled "yes of course!" they exclaimed. The woman left as silently as she came. The bell shrilled for afternoon classes and the girls walked up the path to class. The bullies were at the door "where have you mongrels been? Trying to hide from us? Oh! how sad!"

Sarah and Janice went into class more peaceful than they had left. "do you feel it?" said Sarah to Janice, "something is different, those bullies did not affect me so much" "Yes" said Janice and smiled. Something inside was stirring and she was not sure.

The next day, the girls went down to the lower lawn at lunch break. This time the woman was there waiting for them. Sarah and Janice beamed to see her. They sat down on the bench and spoke gently. The woman spoke of her quiet life in the village nearby. The girls lived in the town which was busier. The woman asked how the girls were feeling? Were the bullies still annoying them? They confided to her what happened when they had returned for afternoon classes. The woman looked sad yet full of compassion. "You see bullies are the ones who usually suffer from very deep problems. They must have some big issues to deal with at home. Pray for them!" Sarah and Janice looked at her and said yes, they would, they would pray the Rosary for them. The woman smiled and said she would appreciate that.

After the end of school, the girls went home and after studies phoned each other so that they could pray the rosary together on the phone. As they prayed, they felt a deep peace and compassion for the bullies. It was also like the woman was smiling at them.

The next day Sarah and Janice walked up to the school door to be confronted by the bullies "oh here they come, the goodie goodies" Sarah looked straight at them "you know Jesus loves you and we are praying for you". The bullies laughed out loud "we don't need your prayers thank you!" the girls continued walking inside quietly and into their class rooms and desks.

At the lunch break the two girls walked down to the lower lawn. Would the woman be there today? She did not say anything yesterday! Sure enough, she was there waiting for them. "Thank you for praying for those girls, I am grateful" Sarah and Janice looked at each other "how could she know this?" "ah well maybe she just guessed that they had prayed for them." Sarah and Janice sat on the bench. The woman remained standing. Suddenly, the other girls came down the path "so this is where you are hiding, you mongrels!

You cannot hide from us forever, we'll find you where-ever you go, you know" "So, who is this? An inspector? Look at her clothes, so old fashioned! Are you tatle - telling on us? You'll pay for it!" the woman looked at the bullies. "No," she said gently, "I am not an inspector, nor Council inspector, you do not know who I am, for your hearts will not allow you to know me" suddenly the woman's clothes began to shine brighter than the sun. It was so bright that Sarah and Janice had to shield their eyes and the bullies covered their faces, turned and ran up the path, screaming in fright.

The woman turned to Sarah and Janice "don't be afraid, I am here for you. She held the girls in her arms and comforted them. I am Miriam, Mary your mother, I am with you always. Those girls will not bother you anymore. Pray for them and I shall take them to my son Jesus. They need his mercy and love." The girls held on to Mary and she held them close under her arms. Gently Mary stroked the girls' heads. It's time for afternoon classes girls. Remember when you pray the Rosary, I am there beside you both, praying to the Father and my Son.

Mary kisses the girls on the forehead and blessed them. She then gently went down the path and disappeared. Sarah and Janice looked at each other totally in awe.

Did that really happen? Were they imagining things? A scent of fresh crushed roses filled the air around them. No! Mary was really there and they had met her these couple of days. Together, holding hands, the girls walked up the path to the school door, smiling and praying. "Sarah, my legs are much better, they don't hurt as much!" cried out Janice. Sarah was happy.

On the steps of the school door, the bullies were there. They did not utter a word, but looked down sheepishly. They looked at Sarah and Janice quietly as they walked past. The scent of the roses lingered after the girls filling the air around them.

CHAPTER FIVE
I FEEL ALONE LORD,
WHERE ARE YOU LORD?

Jimmy was a blind man, made blind from fire and metal sparks in his eyes when working in a car factory. He had lifted his visor for a few minutes when sparks from his friend working on a car nearby flew into his eyes. From then on, his eyes had not only deteriorated but he ended up blind. Now, he was living in the ground floor apartment by himself, quite comfortable, with his guide dog Max, a golden retriever. He could navigate himself around the apartment well enough, but he needed Max and his stick when he went out. The people in the area knew Jimmy well and Max was friendly with them all, he knew his master was safe with them.

Every morning Jimmy woke up and listened to the daily news on the local radio station. He would hear the weather forecast and then dressing accordingly he would go out taking his stick and Max with him. As he walked out of the door, Max would sniff the air outside and the surrounding area and gently lead Jimmy outside. Jimmy would also feel his way with his stick hitting the walls and curb as he walked along. Both Max and Jimmy walked at an even pace suited to each other. Max was Jimmy's eyes, his senses. Even though Jimmy's other senses, especially that of hearing had sharpened, Max was alert at every sound and movement around them as they walked.

So, every morning Jimmy and Max went out, did some very basic shopping. All the neighbours and shopkeepers helped Jimmy with the shopping and delivered the goods to his home.

As the seasons changed, Jimmy became older and so did Max. Max was no longer the vibrant dog he was in his younger years. He would, many a time, especially in winter take a while to walk out of the front door. Jimmy would worry and phone the vet often. The vet told him there was nothing to worry about for Max was a strong dog. Jimmy know how much he needed Max for not only was he his guide dog but his best friend also. They knew each other's needs for they were so sensitised to each other.

It was autumn when Jimmy felt the cool air and decided that a walk in the park would be a great idea for both him and Max. He'd pack a lunch for the two of them and walk through the park. Jimmy could feel the crunch of the autumn leaves beneath his feet and smell the damp of the autumn rain on the leaves and soil. So, Jimmy woke up. Max awoke somewhat sluggishly "come on boy, let's go out this morning, it's fresh outside, it'll do us good!" Max stood on his four feet, stretched, wagging his tail and waited for his breakfast. "here you go" said Jimmy pouring his dried food in his doggy bowl. Max ate dried food in the morning and soft food in the evening, that way he kept his system going and running well.

As Max ate his food Jimmy ate a sandwich and prepared sandwiches to take with them. He'd have to prepare something special for Max, dried food with some meat. When all was ready, Jimmy put on his coat, tied up Max's collar and lead, collected his stick from the stick holder and began to walk out. When they reached the outside, Max began to smell the air looking around him.

He needed to see if all was clear and safe for Jimmy. They began to walk. Crossing roads, Max would hear and see the green safety cross light and guide Jimmy across the road. Since most of the people who drove in the area recognized both Max and Jimmy, they were cautious when they saw them, giving them the chance to cross safely.

Once in the park they walked gently through the paths and over the grass savouring the smell of the leaves and damp soil. Max lay down often rolling in the grass since he loved it so much. Jimmy would laugh. How he loved it when his beloved dog enjoyed it. Max was like a son to him, a best friend. Jimmy and Max were inseparable. Max knew when Jimmy was out of sorts and would bark in such a way that the neighbour and landlady, Mrs Flora who had a spare key, would come to check in on him.

As autumn progressed and Jimmy and Max enjoyed their walks in the park trampling over the fallen leaves and smelling the dew sodden ground. Max became quieter and this worried Jimmy. He phoned the vet, who once again assured him that all was ok, but to make sure he would come to visit Max.

One day as Autumn was turning into winter Jimmy wanted to walk in the park before the cold and snow set in. He went towards the door. Max would by now been bounding up and ready to go out, to have breakfast before. But Max did not stir. Jimmy walked his way over slowly to where Max was and knelt down and shook him. Max stirred slightly and growled quietly. Jimmy was startled. He began to shout out for Flora. She came down quickly and opened the door. She saw Jimmy on the ground over Max. "Mrs Flora, I think Max is sick, please call the vet quickly." Mrs Flora called the vet, Dr Mark Hammond. He was coming over immediately.

Dr Mark Hammond came and quickly checked Max. "We have to get him to the animal hospital immediately." He said. He called for the animal ambulance.

They carried Max out on a stretcher. Mrs Flora held Jimmy's hand. "He'll be ok Jimmy, now you see" she said trying to comfort him. Max was taken to the animal hospital. Jimmy sat down with his head buried in his hands "can I make you a cup of tea Jimmy dear?" asked Mrs Flora. "no thank you, I don't think I can stomach anything at the moment!" replied Jimmy. Time passed, 1 hour, 2 hours, then the phone shrilled. Both Jimmy and Mrs Flora jumped up startled.

"Please take the phone Mrs Flora." Mrs Flora answered the phone and spoke in monosyllables "hmm, yes Dr Hammond, I see Dr Hammond. Would you like to speak to Jimmy?"

Mrs Flora passed the phone to Jimmy "Dr Hammond wants a word with you, better sit down." Jimmy took the phone "Jimmy, I am sorry but I have sad news for you. Max was not at all well. He had heart and kidney failure, we had no choice but to put him out of his misery and put him down. He would not have survived" Jimmy's face went white and dropped the phone from his hands "Jimmy! Jimmy!" cried Dr Hammond from the other end. Mrs Flora sat next to Jimmy who began to weep. She picked up the phone "I'll take care of him Dr Hammond. Thank you for everything, you did your best, Jimmy knows that." With that Mrs Flora returned the phone to its cradle. Jimmy was sobbing. "My best friend, he's gone and now I am all alone. I am all alone Lord, where are you Lord?"

Mrs Flora tried to comfort him as much as she could. "you have us, your friends with you, we care for you" she assured him. That was not enough for Jimmy.

"Yes, thank you but Max was here with me, we were inseparable." He continued to weep. Mrs Flora got up "I'll bring you some hot soup later this evening ok."

When she left, Jimmy got up and walked cautiously towards his bedroom. He knelt at his bed and wept. "Why Lord, Why? I am all alone now Lord, where are you Lord?" In the meantime, word had travelled about Max and Jimmy. All the neighbours were worried and concerned about Jimmy.

In the coming days boxes of food and various deliveries were made to Jimmy to help him in his dilemma, though he was grateful, it did nothing to alleviate his loss.

Mrs Flora came and spoke to Jimmy. "Let's take Max's stuff out and wash out his bed, shall we?" the smell of Max kept on reminding Jimmy of his presence. Reluctantly Jimmy agreed. Mrs Flora washed down the flat and gave it a good clean. There was dog's hair fluff everywhere, on the sofas, bedcovers and clothes. She had to brush everything down, air all the coverings and wash Jimmy's clothes that were smelling of Max. One day, there was a commotion outside Jimmy's door. Mrs Flora came and opened the door, calling out for Jimmy who made his way from the bedroom to the front door. "Jimmy there are your friends here to see you!" she said.

Many people entered the front room of the flatlet but a special guest came in. He went upto Jimmy and began to sniff him up and down. Jimmy held out his hand and the dog licked his hand, smelling him. Jimmy laughed and patted the dog on the head, "and who is this?" "this is Jack, he's for you, we have bought him for you, a fully trained guide dog. He's a black Labrador". They undid the leash and Jack went around the flatlet smelling and sniffing everything. "We have brought you new bedding for Jack." Jack bounced up and down, happy. Jimmy did not know what to say. He was so very happy "come Jack boy, come!" Jack came and jumped on Jimmy "woah boy, woah!" Jack slurped all over Jimmy's face. "we'll do well you and I Jack" "come boy would you like some doggie treats, they belonged to my Max, but he's gone now, you are here so you can enjoy them."

Jimmy thanked his friends for their immense love and dedication. He was overjoyed. That night before Jimmy went to sleep, he called Jack to his bedside to say their night prayers, just as he would with Max. "Thank you Lord for your goodness to us, thank you Lord for giving me Jack. I have a friend. Thank you, Lord!" Jack looked up at him as though to affirm the prayer.

They both huddled. Needless to say, that Jack did not sleep in his own bed that night but slept at the bottom edge of Jimmy's bed. He was going to look after his master morning and evening. The two of them slept well and woke refreshed the next day to start their adventures together.

CHAPTER SIX
HELP ME TO BELIEVE LORD,
WHERE ARE YOU LORD?

Michael ran out of the door of his grandfather's house, tears streaming down his face. Why Lord, Why? The doctor had come and given them the dreaded news that grandpa Joe was badly sick and may not last long. Many years ago, Michael, who was about ten years old then, had witnessed the death of his parents in a tragic accident. His parents had just dropped him off at school when a transport truck hurtled into them, killing them both instantly, the car was left mangled. This was five years ago. It was grandpa Joe who had come and taken Michael under his wing. Together they would go fishing in the nearby river, fishing for salmon that swam upstream to spawn and for rainbow trout. They would walk quietly in the woods nearby, with the sun shimmering through the top branches talking and singing the praises of God. Their lives were serene. Michael continued to go to school and had to study hard for he wanted to enter into the nearby technical school as he wanted to become a mechanical engineer. This would help his grandpa on the farm. But now this happened, just out of the blue.

Michael was not only angry but had lost all faith. What kind of a God was he? Michael ran out and into the nearby meadows where the cows grazed peacefully and the sheep on the hilltops did not stir but continued their daily business of grazing and sleeping. They seemed indifferent to his raging and troubled heart, faith in God.

First, he had taken his parents and now he was about to take grandpa Joe.

He ran to the great oak tree in the middle of the meadow, a tree where he loved to come and listen to the birds in the branches. But now he felt so forlorn that they did not cheer him up at all, but were rather a disturbance to his sorrowful heart.

"Lord, where are you? Help me to believe Lord. Don't take grandpa Joe away, you don't need him, I do. Help me to believe Lord, help me!" Michael began to sob, crying out for his mother and father. Slowly, the boy lay down and fell asleep.

Michael heard a voice calling him through his sleep, "Michael! Michael!" Michael stirred slightly. A man stood in front of him, with light shining behind him. He was gently caressing his head. "Your parents are not dead, but very much alive, they are here with me!" Michael was a bit more awake now "that's not possible, they died, I saw them, I went to their funeral, they are dead I tell you, not alive!"

"No Michael! they are alive, come, see" Michael could see two shadows come out from the light – slowly, he was able to distinguish their silhouettes. It was his parents – Michael shouted for joy, mummy, daddy you are here!" "Yes" said the man "I told you they are alive, for with death, life does not end, but changes. They are alive and with me, not on earth." Michael was still in a daze and felt very much asleep. Was this a dream, or was it for real?

"What do you want me to do for you Michael?" "Please Lord, help me to believe that Grandpa Joe will be ok, that you will not have to take him to you yet."

The man stood upright in front of Michael "Michael, I am Jesus, do you believe in me?" "Yes, Lord I do believe, help me to believe more" Jesus knelt down again and held Michael's head in his arms, cradling him. "All will be ok Michael! all will be ok."

Michael lay down again and fell asleep. He must have slept for quite a long time for he suddenly woke up with the sun setting over the hilltops. He quickly stood up and began to run back to Grandpa Joe's house. Rushing through the door, he stopped short.

Grandpa Joe was sitting in his usual armchair with a bowl of soup in his hands.

Martha, the housekeeper was there, smiling and briming with joy. "well you never Michael, suddenly your grandpa Joe was well, he got up and asked for his favourite soup." Michael looked incredulously at them. "But when did this happen?" he asked. Grandpa Joe looked at Michael, "Son I was so bad, then suddenly this man, I knew it was Jesus immediately, stood in front of me, held my head in his arms and spoke my name gently. He stayed with me a while and asked me if I believed in him? I answered who are you that I should believe in in you and he said I am Jesus. Then I knew Michael, that all was going to be ok. Jesus came to heal me and I am here, Michael, with you."

Michael began shouting for joy, jumping up and down. "Thank you, Jesus, Thank You!" He told grandpa Joe and Martha what had happened to him. All three of them looked at each other in amazement. In their hearts they knew the Lord was faithful, but sadly their faith had waned a bit. They had never experienced such intimacy with the Lord, especially after the death of Michael's parents before, but now things had changed. The Lord Jesus had shown them that he was always with them no matter what.

All three of them knelt down on their knees giving thanks to the Lord for his goodness, love and mercy.

Never a day went by when grandpa Joe and Michael did not pray or thank the Lord for his goodness. Grandpa Joe and Michael continued their walks in the woods and fishing in the river. The fish seemed to jump and dance around with them. Martha continued her baking and cooking in the house. They remembered their heartfelt cry "Help me to believe Lord" and yes, he had done that, even if it was through pain and suffering, the Lord had brought them to the place of deeper faith and belief in him, Jesus.

CHAPTER SEVEN
I CANNOT UNDERSTAND,
WHERE ARE YOU LORD?

Annie and Martin had prayed and prayed for a child. After two years married, they were still childless. Yet both of them believed in the power of prayer and in the Lord's goodness and faithfulness. One day after checking a pregnancy test, Annie found out she was with child. Both of them were delirious and happy, dancing and jumping up and down for joy. "Thank you, Lord, Thank you." Martin immediately began to take good care of Annie, making sure she had her rest and good food. He took over most of the chores in the home for he did not want Annie to exert herself in anyway. They wanted to care for the little one she was carrying. When the time came to visit the doctor, all seemed ok and the ultrasounds were fine. The heart beat was regular and the baby was forming and growing well. Both Annie and Martin took ultrasound photos of their little child. Did they want to know the gender of the child? Neither of them were particular at all, all they wanted was that the child was healthy, safe and sound.

One day after the routine visit to the doctor, they noticed a certain frown on the doctor's face. "What is it Dr Mackenzie?" asked Martin rather worried "I don't like the look of the back of the baby, maybe we should have further tests done" said Dr Mackenzie. Both Martin and Annie froze in fear. "what kind of tests?" they asked "oh just blood tests, sample tests from the amniotic sac!" he replied.

Martin and Annie returned home not elated but fearful. What was happening. The tests had been set for the following day. Together

Annie and Martin sat in their living room and prayed, they prayed for their little one and for faith knowing that the Lord could only bring good out of this.

The next day Martin took Annie into the clinic for the tests. As such they were nothing serious, blood tests were taken from Annie and fluid was removed from the sac. More ultrasounds were taken. These were sent to the laboratory for diagnosis.

Annie and Martin returned home, fearful and worried. Again, they prayed trusting in the Lord's love and mercy.

That afternoon, Martin's mobile rang, it was Dr Mackenzie. "Martin, the situation is quite grave, your child has a problem in the spine. It can be dealt with if we start from now" He began to explain the situation. Martin froze " Yes, Yes of course. Dr Mackenzie."

How was Martin going to tell Annie? He sat her down gently and explained the situation to her. Annie broke down in tears, after these years of waiting, then this! "Why Lord Why? I cannot understand Lord, Where, are you Lord?"

Dr Mackenzie suggested they visit a certain specialist who dealt in these cases. It was in his opinion that the child would not be operated whilst still in the womb, that was a possibility which was for them to decide.

After seeing the specialist both Annie and Martin decided to wait until the birth of their child. They now took more than extra care and their maternity visits were more regular.

Buying the requirements for the newborn were not such a joy as it should have been. Martin did not want Annie to feel dejected, he was positive and interjected what fun they were going to have with their little one.

Both Martin and Annie opted for a Caesarean section birth since this would reduce any strain on the child. Finally, the day came when they had to go into the clinic. Dr Mackenzie was there with his nurse and midwife. He continued to assure them that all was going to be ok. Martin could be with her, covered by a screen and if Annie wanted, she too was able to see her child coming into the world.

The procedure was quick, and the little one was born. A boy, who screamed and cried letting everyone know that he had arrived. The doctor quickly took him inside to check him. He could see the problem in the back, they would deal with that in the next few hours.

John was a vivacious boy, always on the go, never really keeping still. His parents worried for him, for even to teach him the rudiments of behaviour were a big problem, for he would become frustrated. He had to learn to walk with difficulty. The various operations he had on his back had been successful, but his parents still worried about him. They had been to several doctors and each one had told them they he would come in time.

John started attending kindergarten and his parents hoped that mixing with other children would help him, but in fact it only made things worse. John would become disruptive. His parents were at their wits end. He would not respond when spoken to especially when his name was called. He would not join in to the birthday parties of the other children in the class, especially with the blowing out of candles and the cutting of the cake. He always wanted to be the centre of attention. One time, if the teacher had not stopped him, he would have tossed the cake over completely. John would hobble over and throw toys around. The teachers tried to stop him but he would rant and rave until everything calmed down.

One day things became so bad that John's parents decided to go to see a specialist, a psychologist who dealt with cases such as John's.

That night she went into John's room and sat at the end of his bed. "Shall I read you your favourite bedside story John?" she asked him. "Yes, please mummy" he said. She looked at her son so lovingly and looked up at the Crucifix over his bed "I cannot understand Lord, help me, where are you? This is too complex and difficult for me Lord, I need you."

When the day of the appointment came, John did not go to Kindergarten but went with his parents to the psychologist. The psychologist had been filled in about John's physical situation and how it was affecting him emotionally and psychologically. It was affecting the whole family and the children at school.

The psychologist looked at the parents directly "quite frankly Mr and Mrs Thompson, it is not John who is the problem, but you both are." Annie and Martin looked at each other and then at the psychologist. "the more you continue to treat John as a victim, the more he is going to act like one and expect to be treated like one. Let him live his life normally, fend for himself, deal with the situations that other children deal with, himself. Allow him to fall and then to get up on his feet, he is quite capable of that. Don't be afraid to correct and discipline him when and where necessary. Also give him chores to do in the home so that he can feel useful, small things. At this age he should be clearing his toys after he plays with them. You cannot be there all the time. How he turns out is up to you" Annie and Martin looked incredulously at each other and at the psychologist. They knew she was right and they had to deal with the situation straight away. Slowly daily life continued. Annie and Martin turned to the Lord in their care of John and tried their best to be good parents. John grew up and went to primary school.

One day on their way home from primary school, they chatted with John in the car. Martin asked John, "hey son how would you like to join a ball team?" John looked at his dad "but dad, I cannot run, are you making fun of me?" "No son, I'll look into it" the next day after school his father collected John and went to the local ball club. There, there were a whole lot of youngsters who hobbled around playing ball, they all seemed to have leg or back disabilities. The coach came up to John, "want to join us? we could do with another on the team." John was delighted and hobbled over as fast as he could "look dad, I'm playing football!" he cried out. John ran and fell. His mother Annie was going to run to him but Martin stopped her. "Let him be, he'll get used to it." John got up and two other members of the team came to see if he was ok. "Sure, I am," he said. "keep moving boys" whistled the coach. The coach came over to John's parents. "Here, he will learn to take the rough and tumble safely. They will learn to play a good game of ball."

On their way home, John could not stop recounting his great time on the field. "and you know what mum, dad, we are having a match and I will probably be playing, isn't that great?"

Annie and Martin were happy. That evening Annie lay quietly next to John "you know John, maybe you know that your situation is not the best, but so long as you can enjoy your life and are not held back, that is what is most important. Remember the Lord is always with us." With that she hugged and kissed her son, switched off the lights and went out. John turned around and thought to himself. No, "it isn't bad at all, I have parents who love me, they are not divorced and I am playing ball! No, it isn't bad at all. Thank you, Jesus, Good night Jesus!"

The day of the match came. All the boys were excited. They had a good attitude, and had completely disregarded their disabilities even in their practice matches, they were not an impediment or a hinderance, but just another obstacle to be conquered in their life. Their playing in a match was all part of the conquest and they were all set.

The game was fairly played, many took a rough tumble. At a point John fell and was kicked badly in his leg. Annie jumped up but Martin held her "let the coach deal with this." He told her. In the changing rooms, Annie and Martin went down to see John "how are you John, are you hurt?" "Mum, don't you worry about me, I can take care of myself, it's a ball game out there, and we are men. We can handle it. Just because I have had a problem and operations on my back doesn't mean I cannot play ball. I'll be ok. It's you who worries too much" Annie looked at her son, John, she suddenly realized that her son was now grown up.

He had conquered his disability and not allowed it to destroy him. She had cried out to the Lord years ago because she did not understand, now she knew. She had to let go, to let her son find his way, even with his disability to find and become the man within him, to find the strength within him to overcome the obstacles in life at such a young age. It was then that Annie knew that John would be able to surmount and move forward into his adult life, despite his physical obstacles, even if she and Martin were not around.

CHAPTER EIGHT
LET ME HAVE HOPE LORD,
WHERE ARE YOU LORD?

What is hope? Lorna kept on asking herself this question over and over again. She delved into the Word of God. She was seeking for answers. Her life was in disarray and she knew that the Lord was speaking to her but she was not sure. As she took notes of the texts and passages, she began to notice a pattern that began to emerge. It was like a silver thread going through the texts. "Give me hope Lord, Let me see Lord, where are you Lord?" She knew that to abide in hope would keep her on the straight and narrow.

For weeks her employer had made her life miserable, she could not continue this way. In a way there was a certain loyalty but in another way she just wanted to walk out. But there was the need to find another job. She prayed and prayed for the door to open.

The Lord always fulfilled his promises. But she could not understand his promises to her. She wanted to, but was not sure. She knew that hope and faith was the confident expectation of what God had promised and its strength lay not in herself but in his faithfulness.

Hope opens the door to faith, she needed to have more faith, to pray more and be ready to walk the road more. What was the Lord asking of her? She knew that she could not place her hope in the material aspects of the world, that would bring disillusion and discontentment. But in her work, she had to remain positive, even though her surroundings were far from being Christian. She had to remain positive in the midst of her hardship. Hope, trust in his love and faithfulness to her. She knew that to hope was to believe that because the Father was at work, He was in control and things would work out, especially when the circumstances seemed otherwise. He kept her calm and peaceful in dire situations. She remembered the times when the Lord had brought her through severe obstacles and in faith overcame the impossible.

Lorna lay her bible down, it opened by itself on Romans. She read it:

"May the God of hope fill you with all joy and peace in believing, so that by the power of the Holy Spirit you may abound in hope." (Rm 15.13). The Lord was speaking to her. She lowered her head and prayed for the Holy Spirit to come that he may abide in her, bring her joy, peace and faith in believing that all would work out.

"Holy Spirit", I want to abound in joy and hope, believing that all things are possible for those who believe. I need you Lord, fill me with Hope from you Holy Spirit." As Lorna sat there, with the Bible in front of her, she felt a burning stir within her. A deep voice that seemed to rise from out of the Bible spoke to her. "Have faith Lorna, you are not alone, hope and believe."

Instinctively Lorna reached out and gently slid her hand over the scripture page, as though caressing it. It was burning.

She rubbed her fingers. She could still feel as though the words had been burned into her hand. She read the text again, this time more gently and conscientiously with her forefinger gliding over each word. Each word burned. She felt the burning go deep into her heart and mind. The Lord was inscribing His Words in her heart and mind. She became excited and had to calm down. Never had she experienced something like this. "Lord you are so faithful, thank you for your faithfulness, I believe in you Lord, thank you Lord."

That night Lorna went to bed peacefully and slept soundly in the knowledge that all was in the Lord's hands.

As Lorna sat in the bus on her way to work the next day, she observed the multitude of people.

What were they thinking? Did they know of the Lord and how he could help them in their lives? Could they truly live their lives without Him? "Lord what do you want of me, how can I serve you in this?"

Lorna arrived at her bus stop and jumped off the bus, thanking the bus driver with a "God Bless you."

She skipped her way to work, somewhat different to the other days when she virtually dragged herself there. As she entered the office, she greeted her colleagues and asked if anyone of them wanted a coffee or croissant from the vending machine. They looked at her

"You're in high spirits today Lorna" said Shirley, her desk neighbour and colleague.

"Yes, I am Shirl, full of the Spirit." She did not think that Shirley would understand the insinuation.

Throughout the day Lorna worked quietly and diligently, always mindful of the Lord beside and within her. She was caring towards her colleagues and actually smiled at her employer even though he was most disagreeable with her.

During her half hour lunch break she went into the recreation room and sat down near the window looking outside. "All those people Lord, what do you want of me Lord?"

She brought out her small bible and looked up the scripture text the Lord gave her. She read it over and over again.

"Lorna, I want you to take this hope to my people, my children who are living without hope in their lives and thus come to faith in me!" Lorna gasped. She had felt the Lord speak deeply within her. This was what he wanted of her. All this time. Now the Lord had brought her to this: "What do I do now Lord?"

Lorna finished her day at work, but instead of catching the bus home, she walked slowly and thoughtfully, going over and over what the Lord had asked of her. How was she to accomplish this? As she walked, she walked past a homeless man. She looked into her bag and brought out some coins. "Here this is for you – have hope, the Lord is with you." She told him "Thank you m'am" he replied. She was about to walk off when she stopped short and turned suddenly. "Excuse me but where do you sleep at night? Is there a shelter for homeless people here abouts?"

"Yes m'am, there is, I go there, but sometimes it is full and they cannot take more people in. It's down Prince's Avenue." Lorna hastily made her way there. She found the place and walked in.

Near the door she saw a woman, probably homeless too "Excuse me, may I speak to someone in charge please?" she asked. "Yes, you can go to Mrs Dumfry's down the corridor then turn to the first green door on your left." Lorna followed the woman's instructions and knocked on the door. "Come in" a woman shrilled inside. Lorna gently opened the door, "excuse me, are you Mrs Dumfry? Hello I am Lorna Appleworth, I don't know, but I feel that the Lord is sending me here. Do you need any help with your work? Mrs Dumfry stood up and cried out "Thank you Lord! I've been praying and praying for extra help with the homeless. These people are desperate, without hope for their future or lives, they need a caring and loving hand. I need help. Yes, most definitely if you can spare the time." Lorna held her bag and sat onto the chair. So, this was where the Lord was leading her. She thought about her work. "Look I have a day job. Is this a paying job or anything?" Mrs Dumfry looked at Lorna, "my dear, the Council looks after our wages, they are not very high I must tell you, about £600.00 a month, but if you can manage with that, why yes it would be wonderful to have you with us." Lorna made her mental calculations regarding her rent and utility bills. Yes, that would cover her costs, just and have a bit left over.

"Mrs Dumfry I would love to join you, but I first have to hand in my notice to my present employer. However, I can come and help you in the evenings after 5.30 if that is ok with you?" Mrs Dumfry was overjoyed. "Let us rejoice and thank God."

"Yes, indeed Mrs Dumfry, for I see that not only has the Lord answered your prayer, but he has answered mine.

CHAPTER NINE

LET ME HELP YOUR NEEDY CHILDREN
WHERE ARE YOU LORD?

Lorna began her work in the shelter. She loved to help the people, listening to them. They would straggle in before nightfall to find a mattress on the ground. Some were lucky to find a bed, but they would all get a hot bowl of thick vegetable soup with meat in it.

As the time wore on and Lorna had given in her resignation from her place of work, she had more time on her hands. During the day, she would go to the baker and buy bread rolls, go home and make sandwiches. She would then take them and give them to the homeless that lay around. So many were so desperate. In her heart she felt the Lord telling her, "poverty is not just those who are without material needs, there are many of my children who are poor!" Lorna listened to the still voice within her "Lord let me see, these people. Let me see, where are you Lord?" Lorna walked and thought. As she thought she prayed. Suddenly it came to her, many people did not know of Jesus Christ, that made them poor, many people were under the domination of drugs and have never known the love of another human being for their own sake. So many social problems.

When she returned to the shelter, she spoke to Mrs Dumfry and asked if she could try to evangelise people in her daily walk in the town. Mrs Dumfry was delighted. "But of course, this is what we are all about dear Lorna".

The next day, Lorna set off with a basket in hand carrying her sandwiches and bottles of water. She stopped and knelt down near the homeless and gave them the bread and bottle of water. She began to speak to them of the love of Jesus. They would look aghast. No-one had ever told them this. She spoke to the drug addicts and alcoholics, giving them the sandwiches and water. As she spoke to them, the said they felt a burning within them. She looked at them and prayed for the Holy Spirit to touch them and strengthen them. Inviting them to come to the shelter at night, she would be there to welcome and care for them.

As time wore on, Lorna realised that she was needed more than full time at the shelter, the people needed her, the soup kitchen was working out well, but more funds were needed. They were not coping with what the Council was giving them. She gathered the homeless together and asked if they were willing to help themselves. Did they know how to sing? Winter and Christmas was drawing near and the people would need warmth, blankets, quilts and shelter. One way or another they began to form a choir. She managed to enrol the help of a singing instructor who began to teach them the rudiments of singing. They were not exactly the Viennese Choir but they managed to coordinate their voices. The time came for Lorna to bring them out into the open.

"My brothers and sisters, I know you understand the importance of what we are doing. Please God this will be appreciated outside". The group of homeless and drug addicts walked gently to the park centre and there set themselves up. Lorna had acquired all the necessary permits from the Local Council.

They gathered and slowly but very nervously began to clear their throats and begin to rehearse the vocal scales. Then the singing began. From a group of homeless people, who had had no hope, from a bunch of drug addicts and alcoholics came out voices that drew people to them. People who heard them from around came to see and hear them. Money was thrown into the baskets they lay on the ground. Lorna had written labels indicating the "Funds for the Shelter of the Homeless". As they sang, joy filled their hearts, their voices lifter higher and higher. Never in their wildest imagination had they thought that they were capable of such a feat. Lorna was thrilled. The Lord had done great things with these people. She was so grateful.

When they had finished, the people applauded and asked if they would come again soon, they would be happy to come and hear them. Lorna told them that these were the homeless from the shelter. The people were amazed for never had they imagined such a thing.

Returning home, the group of people were so excited, they begged Lorna to have another vocal concert for Christmas, this time, they could have it at the shelter, or even the Council Hall. Lorna said she would ask. Counting the money, the people had given them, they managed to cover the costs and more, they would care for more homeless and those in need. Bathrooms and showers were needed. The word went round and more drug addicts, homeless and alcoholics came to the shelter for help.

Lorna knew that the time had come for her to be available to them full time. She decided after praying for discernment and discussing the subject with Mrs Dumfry, to sell her apartment and come and live with the homeless. She would become as one of them, living with them and caring for them there. She knew she was doing the right thing, for a joy filled her heart and a deep peace engulfed her.

With the proceeds from the sale of her flatlet, Lorna built showers and toilets in the Shelter, a new kitchen, beds and mattresses, blankets. She wanted her family to have all they needed.

Now they began to prepare for Christmas. The Council approved her request to use the Council Hall. The music instructor trained the group even further.

They were going to sing and sing Christmas Carols.

On the day, the Hall was filled to overflowing. All proceeds from the tickets were to be for the shelter. The group sang and sang, joy ringing from their hearts. One of them even gave a solo rendition of Away in a Manger. The hall was silent and felt the awe around them.

At the end of the concert, everyone congratulated Lorna for the immense work done. She refused any praise but looked at the group and gave all thanks to God. "This is his work. He is the One who gave hope to those who had no hope".

Fr Matthew, parish priest at St Vincent Church came upto Lorna and asked if they would be interested to sing Christmas Carols in his Church over the Christmas period. The group were excited and begged to be able to do so. Lorna agreed and together they all arranged for the times they were able to come. With the money they had been receiving as donations, the homeless were now able to buy decent clothes and feel the dignity that was due to them as children of God.

"Lorna", they said, "we would never have been able to do this without you, never have reached this far without you". "You believed and hoped for us, when we had left all hope behind".

Lorna, remembered that time when she was in the bus on her way to work, looking out of the bus and asking the Lord the people she saw had any hope, if she could give them hope.

She looked at her new family and said "it is not I who has given you hope or your dignity back, but Jesus. Thank him. If He in his mercy has used me at all it is only out of his love for you".

She looked at them gently and tenderly. "It's late my brothers and sisters, time to go back to the shelter".

They walked out in the cold night air and quietly hummed their Christmas carols on their way home.

CHAPTER TEN

SHOW ME HOW TO LOVE AGAIN LORD, WHERE ARE YOU LORD?

Matthew glanced at the girl across the tables, she always came in at the same time 12.45pm. She would come in at lunch time. As he observed her, he noted how she would place her hair behind her ears and would eat her soup gently. It would be her lunch break. He could not stir up the courage to go and speak to her, he was basically a very withdrawn person and he could not even imagine how he would feel if she would just turn him away.

A few just over a year ago, his previous girl friend had walked out on him, and he was still stinging from the experience. She had told him, out of the blue, that she was seeing someone else and wanted their relationship to end. Naturally, Matthew was hurt and taken aback. So, all this time she had been pretending to love him. He raised his eyes to look at the girl who sat but a few tables away. Could he and would he be able to love again. He was afraid to love for fear of being hurt again. He was afraid to show his emotions or even any interest at all. It would be better to forget it altogether.

Matthew finished his burger and coffee quietly, he looked up and thought he caught the girl's eye, she quickly lowered her eyes, smiling. No! he was imagining things. He got up and walked to the cash counter to pay for his meal and began to walk out. Outside he glanced inside, the girl was paying at the cash desk and began to walk out. Matthew was so nervous, what was he to do? Should he stop and talk to her, Lord what do I do? She came out of the door and smiled at him. She looked at him "sorry for being intrusive but I seem to know you somewhere, maybe at university or higher secondary?" she held out her hand "I am Janice Longford, pleased to meet you." They shook hands lightly. At the mention of that name, Matthew's mind went into a whirl, Janice Longford? Goodness she was the very plain girl in higher secondary and now she was a beautiful swan! "Wow yes I remember, it was in higher secondary I think, wonderful to see you again. Hope you are doing well?" "Do you come here often?" "Yes, I do," she replied "I come for my lunch break. I work as an interior designer with Crouts Interiors Ltd nearby, how about you?"

Matthew looked up and smiled, "I'm an accountant with Johnson and Johnson Accountants. I too come here for my lunch. I need to get away from my desk." Smiling, they parted company and returned to their work.

As Janice and Matthew returned home, they both mused on their encounter with each other. Janice found him attractive, but she was very scared of creating any form of relationship. Her parents were divorced. It was a long and traumatic battle. Janice was only 9 at the time, it had affected her tremendously. No! Marriage was not for her.

She would not consider any form of intimate relationship outside marriage, that was against her principles and faith. Janice wanted a family but also only with a man that could be relied on. A sturdy man who had the same principles she had, they would have a family together and bring them up together. "Lord does this kind of man exist?" she asked. No answer seemed to come her way, so she threw herself into her work.

Matthew returned home and opened the cupboard where he kept some old photo albums. He searched for the one of his high school year, he found it and looked for Janice Longford. Yes, there she was, long straggly hair. She was so well groomed now, well-polished. He looked and gazed at the photo. "Lord is it possible?" Closing the album, he put it aside and allowed himself a stiff drink.

The next day Matthew was more determined than ever to meet up with Janice during their lunch break. It would not be anything planned, just a happy coincidence. He went to the usual pub and was rather disappointed when he did not find her there. After sitting down and ordering his burger, Janice came in. "Hi nice to see you again, it seems we like the same haunts."

"Hi" said Matthew, hoping he sounded very casual. He like her air of confidence, for it helped him to overcome his shyness. Over the following days both Matthew and Janice would casually meet up at lunch time in the local pub for their lunch break. Their discussion inevitably wound around their work and often hobbies, she liked homely things and he liked sports. They were both very busy people so their social life was somewhat limited.

As Matthew returned home one evening, his bus went past a very quaint Italian Trattoria. He quickly disembarked from the bus and went into the restaurant to have a look. It was quiet, with typical Italian table ware and the music was not the type that deafened you, so one was able to have a decent conversation. He had a quick look at the menu. Yes, it seemed favourable with a good choice. Musing on what he saw, Matthew was hoping to ask Janice out for a meal one evening, if she agreed of course. So, he decided to have his supper there. He wanted to try out the food, wine and of course the service. Matthew was still unsure due to his previous experience, but he knew he could not stay in the cupboard forever. He liked Janice and felt good with her, he felt safe. She brought out the good in him and he liked that.

The next day over their lunch break, Matthew broached the question, clearing his throat.

"Would you like to come out for a simple dinner with me one of these evenings? There is a quaint Italian Trattoria nearby, Giorgio. I've eaten there and the food seems to be very good." Janice smiled "Why Yes Matthew, I'd love to come. It'll be great and I love Italian pasta." "Wonderful shall we make it for Friday evening around 7.30, I'll book a table for 2" said Matthew.

That evening both Janice and Matthew thought about the other. Janice liked Matthew, he seemed sturdy, a man with his head on his shoulders, not one of these flirty, Adonis type of men. "Lord if he is the one, then show me? Show us, bring this forward Lord that we may see your way in our lives. I am afraid to love Lord, where are you Lord?"

Matthew too began to pray and asked the Lord for the way forward "Lord you know I am afraid to love again. I don't want to be hurt again. If this is not to be, then don't let it start. I like her and if I fall in love with her and it is then off, I shall be devastated. Lord I am afraid to love, where are you Lord?"

Matthew booked the table at Giorgio's. After work both Matthew and Janice walked quietly, hardly saying a word, through the park to the Trattoria. It was a tranquil night, brisk. The moon was out, shimmering through the trees. The whole area looked very romantic. "Are you cold?" asked Matthew "No, I'm not thank you" replied Janice "Its beautifully fresh and brisk, one can smell the earth and the leaves in the damp."

They arrived at the Trattoria, Giorgio himself welcomed them and showed them to their table. "I will bring you the best Table wine from La Sicilia, my family, they make the wine the old way and send me bottles in boxes, but today I want you to be my guests and to have this bottle, on the house, on Giorgio." Matthew and Janice beamed. "Thank you." Giorgio opened the wine and poured out a bit, "Hmmm, the bouquet, taste sir, the flavour, fruity but not sweet, dry and good for pasta or anything else you might wish to eat." "Maybe, la Signorina would like to have some too? You will surely like it."

Giorgio brought them the menus. They ordered their meal, laughing and talking. They enjoyed the wine and the food. They enjoyed each other's company. As the evening wore on, the restaurant had to close, they were the last to leave. Giorgio offered them an aperitif – "perhaps a Fernet Branca, that settles the stomach before you go to sleep, please it is from Giorgio."

Matthew and Janice walked out of the Trattoria relaxed. The air was much chillier now, they wrapped their coats around them. "I'll see you home Janice." Matthew signalled for a taxi and quickly saw Janice to her flat. He got out of the taxi but did not make an approach upon her. He just kissed her on the cheek. "Thank you for such a wonderful evening Matthew." Janice went up the stairs and opened the door of the apartment building and went inside.

Matthew returned into the taxi "25 Walnut Grove please" he asked the driver. In the car, Matthew thought about their evening together. It was a lovely and comfortable evening. He was glad he did not make any advance on her as that would have spoiled it all. He would have to take it slowly.

Janice thought about Matthew. He was a gentleman. She liked the way he kept his presence and did not push himself upon her. She felt good about it all.

Over the weekend, they both continued their weekend routines, however thinking about each other.

The coming week, they again met up at the pub over lunch. It virtually became a ritual. Janice would have her soup and Matthew, a burger or pie.

Again, Matthew asked Janice if she would come to Giorgio's. She willingly agreed, but only if this time she tabbed the bill. Matthew was going to disagree. Janice insisted. She enjoyed going out with him and if they wanted to continue their Friday evenings out then they would have to take it in turns to tab the bill, it was only fair, she said. Matthew had to agree, if that made her happy.

For the next 2 months they continued to go to Giorgio's on Friday evenings. Their conversation then began to turn to the future. What were their interests in settling down? Their ideas on family life? They both realised the importance of the Lord in their lives and how they prayed and built their lives upon him. Both Matthew and Janice found that they held a great compatibility in their ideas regarding family life and how work was to be juggled with family. Janice accepted the fact that if she had children, she would not be able to work the way she was doing now, however she did say she would be able to work from home.

Over time, both Matthew and Janice began to think in terms of greater friendship. One evening when Matthew took Janice home, he got out of the taxi and instead of kissing her on the cheek, he kissed her properly. "Janice, I love you." He told her. She looked at him so endearingly "So do I Matthew."

The following Friday as they sat down to eat at Giorgio's, Matthew asked Giorgio to lower the lights. Quietly he put his hand in his pocket and brought out a small box. Opening the box, there lay a shimmering diamond engagement ring. Matthew stood up and kneeling on one knee "Janice I am asking you, to do me the honour of accepting me to be my wife. I offer you all my heart and love, my life and all that I can give you." Janice looked at Matthew and began to cry "Matthew, of course I'll marry you!" she stood up and flung herself into his arms. Giorgio was totally emersed in the whole situation "Che amore, che bello, Festegiamo! We shall celebrate my dear friends! Vieni, a la grande bella copia!" Come my friends I bring out my best Proseco, we shall celebrate this happy occasion. That evening they decided to walk home. One the way they talked of how they had both prayed to the Lord to help them in this their relationship, the both confessed how afraid they were to love, yet looking at each other they knew that with the Lord they would make it through. As they walked, they felt a gentle breeze flowing through the trees. Around the corner they came to a small chapel, quite cut off from the common road. They decided to see if it was open. They went inside and kneeling down gave thanks to the Lord for their love and for the courage to open their hearts to the beauty that the Lord had given to each one of them, to be discovered one by the other. In the silence they allowed the Spirit of God to embrace them and to allow their love to be more cemented in him. A peace descended and quiet enfolded the chapel. They were in the Presence of God. Their love was being cradled in his heart and they knew he would always be with them no matter what.

CHAPTER ELEVEN

HELP ME LORD TO UNDERSTAND
THE SACREDNESS OF LIFE,
WHERE ARE YOU LORD?

Anna paced the floor of her flatlet, she had a relationship with her boyfriend and she just took a pregnancy test. She was now very worried that she might be pregnant. Her friends and even Jerome, her boyfriend said she was to have an abortion should she become pregnant. She was very nervous. "Please Lord don't let me be pregnant!" she looked at the test, the result was positive – Damn. She was pregnant. What was she to do? Everything inside her screamed. She just did not want this child, she was angry. She had to work and finish college at the same time. Her work supported her as well as her college fees. There were bills to be paid and she for certain could not afford to keep and take care of a child.

Hesitantly she picked up her phone and dialled Jerome's number. It was engaged. She felt relieved. She knew she could not put it off. She then phoned her best friend Marilou. "oh no Anna, you must have that abortion, I will come with you and arrange it myself my dear!" Anna was scared. She dare not tell her mother or father.
She tried to phone Jerome again, his picked up and sounded nervous.

"Jerome, is all ok? I have something to tell you. I've had the pregnancy test, and it's come out positive. I am pregnant!" Anna took in a deep breath

"NO! it's not ok and you can forget me forking out for the child". "I told you, if you become pregnant you must have an abortion, you should be on the contraception pill".

Anna sat down, shocked. She never expected this reaction from Jerome.

"But it's your child Jerome".

"Forget it Anna, it's off, our relationship is off".

Anna held her stomach and began to weep.

"Stop this Anna, this won't change anything. Go and deal with this yourself at the abortion clinic".

Anna put down the phone and went into her room to lie down. She wept and wept. What had happened. Jerome said he loved her, but now she felt used. This child, unwanted and very much a mistake, created havoc in their relationship and now Jerome was blaming her.

As she lay there, she remembered her mother nursing her little brothers and sisters. They were such a happy family. She would be shocked if Anna told her about contemplating an abortion, yet on the other hand she could not bring up this child.

Still crying Anna got up and opened her drawers, searching for some old family photos. She found a few when they were young. On her chest of drawers was an old statuette of Mary holding the Child Jesus.

Anna cried out loud, "this cannot be, I cannot deal with this, yet on the other hand I cannot have an abortion. Lord help me to understand the sacredness of life. Where are you Lord in all of this?"

Furtively Anna searched for her old Rosary beads. She had not prayed the Rosary in a long time. Before she began to pray, she called out to Mary. "Mary you became with child before you were married to Joseph, help me in this. I do not feel it is right to have an abortion, I don't want to, even though Jerome and my friends think I should, but I don't. Help me". Quietly Anna began to pray. As she prayed, a peace descended upon her, she felt enveloped in motherly love, Mary's presence was with her. She clutched her stomach. "Little one, I will take care of you. I will not abort you, for your life is sacred as much as mine is. Somehow we shall manage". As a family they knew the meaning of sacrifice and caring. Her parents had many children and their father worked hard to support them. Never did they allow the lack of respect of the sacredness of life to waiver from them. When her mother was pregnant with her 3rd child, Anna's brother Jason, he was younger than Anne, from the early stages of the pregnancy the ultrasounds indicated that the child was going to have a strong sclerosis of the back. The doctors advocated abortion. It was in the second trimester of her pregnancy. Her parents were horrified and would not even contemplate the idea. Her father had said. "No! God will provide! We will manage one way or another. This child is sacred and unto God". Now her brother Jason, though he was disabled and had to move around in a wheel chair, became a great lawyer having studied at college and law school. He entered into politics in the Christian Democratic party, and was on the front line in defending the rights of the unborn child. He would be devastated had he to learn that Anna contemplated an abortion. "No" she thought, "God will see me through this".

As Anna's pregnancy continued, her friends kept on insisting on her having an abortion. After all she could still have it until the last trimester of her pregnancy. Jerome did not want to have anything to do with Anna nor the child, he had made that clear. When he found out that she was not going to have the abortion, he made it very obvious that he was, in no way going support her or the child. She had to make her way herself. Anna felt that in fact she had not lost anything, for in this Jerome showed up his true colours. She wanted to care for her child. God would provide.

Now it was time to tell her family. She was due to go home for a short weekend break. As she drove up the drive, her father and mother rushed out to meet her. Seeing her and her bulging stomach they stopped short. There were no questions, but gently her mother guided her inside. Anna told them all that had happened and how and why she refused to have an abortion. Her brothers and sister came home and after the initial surprise of their sister's pregnancy, they began to coo and fuss over her. When her brother Jason came home with his wife and greeted his sister. Upon seeing her condition and learning of her situation, he not only congratulated her but admired her for her strong decision not to run from her obligations and responsibilities to her child, he and his wife would stand by her. She had done the right thing. Her father held Anna close and told her not to worry, they would help her and be with her through this. Slowly over the weekend they began to make plans for the child's birth, the things they had to buy. Anna felt safe in the love and cradle of her family. This is what family was all about. Jerome would never have been able to give her this, or be this kind of a father to the child.

As she slept at night, she held her baby bump in her arms and sang a lullaby. The child stirred within. Anna felt a deep sensation of love and life. She knew she would be a good mother to her child. She would love it and care for it the way her mother had loved and cared for them all. Her father had decided that he was going to buy her the pram and cradle for the little one. Would she be willing to come return home and have the baby here, to return home would mean to forego her preferred college but she could go to the St Ambrose nearby, this was so that they could all look after and help her with the child? Anna was deliriously happy. Yes, she wanted her child to grow up in the kind of love and environment she was used to. This was a big blessing. She knew that all would be alright and her child would be loved and care for. She thanked the Lord for giving her the understanding of the sacredness of life, for she had lived it in her family and was now passing it on to her child.

THE CHILD IN THE WOMB

In the stillness of the night and in a cry, man is conceived, his form taking shape deep within the womb of woman. Yet as the child grows no-one but the Lord perceives that nature and glory hidden within the created vessel. The soul and spirit beat in unison, the heart is touched by the gentleness of life. I stretch and reach out, I am created and grown.

You are grown, my child, yes you are grown, the waves and experiences of life causing ravines in the heart and soul. In silence you watch the world around you, trying as best you can to find your place. You speak and smile yet your eyes and expressions betray the depth of pain within. You search and reach out to be understood and held within a heart that loves and sees. 'Quo Vadis I,,Lord' you cry. Alone, a loneliness so very deep that it plummets you to the depths of your being. Alone, searching, crying, a cry so silent, longing to be heard yet no voice comes out. No words can articulate or express what is deep within. You reach out hoping to grasp an outstretched hand, a friendly and loving hand. Your fears inundate you and you hold your clothes around you fearing your nakedness and vulnerability. Like hungry wolves the crowds tear at you leaving you exposed to the storms and torrents of life. No-one stops to ask of you, they take from you, one after the other, leaving you naked and hungry for love and comfort.

You return to what you know is safe, the womb of she who bore you. Yet you are beckoned to grow and become. In pain you cry out in the birth pangs of the new life borne within. To enter into that transcendence that is all new and light.

In silence you weep, your tears gushing from a heart so wounded, soaking the earth and like a torrential river finding its way to the foot of the Cross. There you rest and let yourself be known. Your Spirit torn and ravaged seeking love.

The Lord's tender words reach out and touch your heart, HIS loving hands take yours and placing them in HIS Heart you behold HIS pain. HIS wounds like the Chrism oil of Baptism, burning, reminding you of who you really are and for what you have been created.

HIS ravaged body on the Cross, eyes tender and beckoning, you reach out hoping to touch and find in HIS wound the balm for your pain. Tears mingled with sweat, HIS torn hands reach into your heart caressing it like a lover. Like the thorns upon HIS brow HE pierces your heart and draws you into HIS pain and suffering that all at once like stormy waves beating upon the shore you enter into the suffering of humanity and experience within you own pain the pain of those who cry, those who cry alone. And in the silence and pain of your own heart you detect and hear the silent cry of your brethren.

The night dark and quiet, and in the moonlight the Wounded One hangs alone. HE beckons 'Come with ME'. As your heart begins to beat in unison with HIS you find yourself, with HIM on the Cross, at peace. Like Him you are born anew.

'Quo Vadis Lord?' 'It is I my child, it is I. I am in your heart on the Cross, you see my child, in you I am not afraid to die, for in you I live.

O LORD, thou hast searched me and known me!

Thou knowest when I sit down and when I rise up;

thou discernest my thoughts from afar.

Thou searchest out my path and my lying down,

and art acquainted with all my ways.

Even before a word is on my tongue,

lo, O LORD, thou knowest it altogether.

Thou dost beset me behind and before,

and layest thy hand upon me.

Such knowledge is too wonderful for me;

it is high, I cannot attain it.

Whither shall I go from thy Spirit?

Or whither shall I flee from thy presence?

If I ascend to heaven, thou art there!

If I make my bed in Sheol, thou art there!

If I take the wings of the morning

and dwell in the uttermost parts of the sea,

even there thy hand shall lead me,

and thy right hand shall hold me.

If I say, "Let only darkness cover me,

and the light about me be night,"

even the darkness is not dark to thee,

the night is bright as the day;

for darkness is as light with thee.

For thou didst form my inward parts,

thou didst knit me together in my mother's womb.

I praise thee, for thou art fearful and wonderful.

Wonderful are thy works!

Thou knowest me right well;

my frame was not hidden from thee,

when I was being made in secret,

intricately wrought in the depths of the earth.

Thy eyes beheld my unformed substance;

in thy book were written, every one of them,

the days that were formed for me,

when as yet there was none of them.

How precious to me are thy thoughts, O God!

How vast is the sum of them!

If I would count them, they are more than the sand.

When I awake, I am still with thee.

O that thou wouldst slay the wicked, O God,

and that men of blood would depart from me,

men who maliciously defy thee,

who lift themselves up against thee for evil!

Do I not hate them that hate thee, O LORD?

And do I not loathe them that rise up against thee?

I hate them with perfect hatred;

I count them my enemies.

Search me, O God, and know my heart!

Try me and know my thoughts!

And see if there be any wicked way in me,

and lead me in the way everlasting!

CHAPTER TWELVE

I AM GRIEVING LORD
WHERE ARE YOU LORD?

Karl carried the box of his office items, flinging them onto the floor. He had just been laid off work. Very politely, he was asked to leave. He knew his work was not up to standard and it had not been so for quite a few months. Since the time of his wife's death, he had dived into a deep depression and no amount of pills or doctors could help him. He came into office, many times unshaven and just sat at his desk. A colleague would bring him a black coffee from the vending machine and he would grab a bite to eat from the canteen. Life was not the same without Doreen. Her smile in the morning, her exuberance and childlike enjoyment of anything small. She was not a demanding person, nor did she need anything big to make her happy. In fact, as he remembered, she hardly ever asked him to buy her things, rather unlike the wives of many of his male colleagues he knew. The children were slowly coming to terms with the going of their mother and he tried as best he could to make it up to them, but he knew he was not able. He was at breaking point and they all needed each other's and help, fast. Karl buried his head into his hands. "Lord what am I to do now? I need to support the family, I am in a depression, where are you Lord? Help us Lord". This deep cry came out from Karl's deepest heart. He just did not know what to do or where to turn. Doreen was not there to comfort him and give him advice. She was always the one to point out some way forward, even when things were at their worst in their marriage and lives in the family. When they were not making ends meet, she went out to work without him realising it and one way or another they made it. She was the strong one and he realised that now. Now she was gone, he felt lost and all alone. No matter what he did, he could not shake off this gnawing depression and feeling of emptiness. He knew he had to not only for his own sake, but for that of his children. What with their mother gone and their father barely there, they were suffering and he knew that. Their school work was suffering and even as children, their childhood was not the same as it was. He was nervous and short tempered. It was affecting everyone. "Doreen, Doreen why did you have to go? Why, Why did that cancer have to take you so treacherously. It did not give us time to understand, to prepare Doreen? Yet you knew, you knew all the time. Why but Why? Lord Why?" This deep grieving rose and with a cry came out of him. He did not even have it in him to be angry, he was just grieving and it would not go away. Not even time to say good bye, for the time was so short. One moment she was at home, fine and preparing meals for the family and the next she was rushed to hospital. She had collapsed during dinner. Karl got up and picked up the files and paper, placing them in the box. He would now go home to a house where he felt desolate. He would have to prepare dinner for the family. He smiled, the children always returned home from school famished. Oh yes that reminded him, he had do the school run and stop to buy from the local small supermarket. He never realised how busy the woman's work was inside the home. His male colleagues would complain that their wives had nothing to do at home. Little did they realise how blessed they were. Their wives were at home caring and keeping home for them, bringing up and caring for the children. He only realised that now and felt bad for never having appreciated Doreen's work in the home enough. She deserved so much more and he did not give it to her. Now it was too late. One thing he could do was try his best for his children, to fill in the empty gap she had left. "Oh Lord I am grieving, where are you Lord?

Karl made his way to his car, threw the box into the boot and started the engine. He first had to call for Kathleen and Jessica and then for Nigel and Timothy. The two girls and boys went to different schools, even though they had different classes. He thanked God that Kathleen was now in her higher secondary as this meant he did not have to spend so much time helping her out with her work yet she needed a lot of attention as she was growing up into a young lady. She missed and needed her mother as a young woman. The others still needed overseeing and though he would be tired, he knew that he had to do it.

He collected the children and stopped over at Green's supermarket to buy the necessary items required. The children had healthy appetites and they took sandwiches with them to school every day. He and Doreen had always insisted that they eat healthy stuff. He deplored the canteen fare the children were offered at school, all deep-fried junk food. It was in no way good for them.

They arrived home. The children jumped out of the car "Hey kids, come and give your dad a hand". They came and the boys carried the shopping into the house, whilst the girls began to unpack the stuff. "Dad, why do you have your office work here? What happened?" Nigel asked. Karl took in a deep breath "hey kids, nothing to worry about, I've been laid off work. Things have not been good since your mother passed away and well, they let me go". The children just starred at him "What are we to do dad?" Nigel and Timothy both piped in "We can get extra jobs dad, working at Green's, that would help out". Kathleen said "I can work at the Sandra's Boutique over the weekend". Karl looked at his children, he was proud of them and he knew their hearts were there to help the family "children, don't you worry, I'll find a job somewhere and somehow. We just have to tighten our belts for a while ok, but we'll make it". The children smiled and ran to their father. Kathleen said "Dad, Jessica and I will prepare dinner, you rest ok. Boys can you lay the table please?"

That night, before Karl went to sleep, he knelt beside his bed and prayed, "Thank you Lord for giving Doreen and myself such wonderful children, I place them in your loving heart and hands. But Lord I am grieving, where are you Lord. I am not only grieving for the loss of Doreen but even for my children. I need a job Lord to support them. They need to feel safe and I am their father". After signing himself with the sign of the cross, Karl felt a deep peace come over him and a sense of a deep voice within him saying "it'll be well Karl, it'll be well!"

CHAPTER THIRTEEN
HELP ME TO BE STILL LORD,
WHERE ARE YOU LORD?

In the previous chapters we have addressed on some of the pain and sufferings that touch people's hearts, maybe they touch yours too. The Lord speaks to our heart and the only way we can hear him is when we are silent, alone with him. Maybe in a quiet chapel or church, or in the country away from the noise of the city. He speaks to our hearts, we just have to be still. Help me to be still Lord, where are you Lord?

I see a heart that is growing and expanding allowing the Lord in, growing in so many ways. A heart that always had so much love in it but needs to know that touch of the potter's hand and to let go, the need of a desert to know oneself and be known.

To cling to him who is our all and allow ourselves to rise above the waves and not be held in by the currents of the day, but to walk on the water and to see things as they truly are and not as we would wish them to be.

The desert removes our tinted glasses and our eyes become accustomed to the glare of the truth, our feet learn to walk not on the smooth tiles but on jagged rocks until they are torn and bleeding and then we can walk on the truth without being torn. We walk sturdily and in strength walk the ways of the Prophets and Patriarchs. We face the beasts and walk on in strength without respect of fear or fervour of man or woman but of the truth no matter how hidden it is, we see it and know it.

Walk this road and let the sages greet you as a sojourner on their path, let your feet be torn and your heart seared with the light of the One who calls and anoints for he is the only one who knows and allows you to be known in HIM.

Think of it and know, be still and know, know him who IS.

He has called you here to be alone with him, to spend some precious time with him, just you and him. You need to know how much he loves and cares for you. Even before he created the heavens and the earth and all there is in it, he knew you and called you by your name, "you see, you are totally mine" say the Lord. "At the right time and place I created your innermost being and placed you in your mother's womb. There I watched over you, was there when you were born and took your first gasping breaths. You were already engraved on the palm of my hand. All the days planned for you were written in my book before even one of them came into being. How precious are my thoughts of you. I know my child there are going to be times of suffering in your life, but do not be afraid for I am with you. It does not compare to the glory to be revealed to you when you come back home to me. How can you say I reject or even abandon you, nothing can ever separate you from my love for you. Whether those in your family and friends hurt you, when in trouble, distress, persecuted or even sin, I can never stop loving you or turn my back from you. Everything that has ever happened or will happen to you, will work for your good because I love you. You have been called according to my purpose and to be formed into the image of my Son Jesus Christ. This is your calling, to be Holy for I am Holy. I created you in my image so that you and I can express love to each other".

"The most intimate relationship you can have is with me, I and you becoming one. Yes, I have called you, with your brothers and sisters here, to become one with me in Jesus. For this I created you, for nothing will ever satisfy your deepest needs and desires, but me. So, my child, seek to know and love me with all your heart and I shall satisfy your heart with love, joy and peace that only I can give. My child if you should fall into sin, turn quickly back, I am so ready to forgive and restore you. Do not let sin separate you from me because then I will have to discipline you as a good father must discipline his child out of love. Even if you have spent a lifetime away from me and are now coming back home, don't be afraid, I am waiting with love for you. I will create in you a clean heart and renew a right spirit in you and restore to you again the joy of my salvation. I will make you willing to obey me and hate sin. Humble yourself therefore under my loving hand, that I may lift you up. I the LORD am compassionate and gracious, slow to anger, abounding in love. I will not accuse you nor harbour anger forever. I do not treat you as your sins deserve or repay you according to your iniquities. My Son Jesus has paid the debt. In His blood you will find all you need to save you from your sins. My Son Jesus has given His life as an atoning sacrifice instead of you.

You see, your sins are all paid for, every single one of them, every pain you have ever or can ever suffer, he suffered. Any depression or rejection, abuse or direct evil, He suffered FOR YOU. Now my little one, just come back and go to the Cross of my Son, stay there a while and let His blood flow over you, cleanse and redeem you for this is My perfect will. When you receive Communion, you receive me for I, your Father, Jesus, my Son and the Spirit are one – you receive the Trinity. The Holy Spirit moves in your life to empower you to love and obey. Let me guide your life according to my plans, for surely I know the plans I have for you, plans for your welfare and not for harm, for a future and a hope. When you call upon me and come and pray to me, I hear you. When you search for me and seek me with all your heart, you will find me. Though the mountains may tremble and the seas roar, my steadfast love will not abandon you. Let my love speak to you, let My Son Jesus redeem you and let the Holy Spirit continue to work in you. For I am with you until the end of time.

I hope these short stories have shed some light upon the current situations we are facing presently, maybe you are facing these situations in your life. Know that the Lord is with you and guiding you. He will never abandon you. Turn to him and let him be your hope and light.

God bless you Sue

Printed in Great Britain
by Amazon